REMEMBERING YOU COMRADE BARDHAN

Conceptualisation
JAYA MEHTA

Editor
VINEET TIWARI

Joshi-Adhikari Institute of Social Studies (JAISS)

REMEMBERING YOU COMRADE BARDHAN

Conceptualisation
JAYA MEHTA

Editor
VINEET TIWARI

Joshi-Adhikari Institute of Social Studies (JAISS)

AAKAR

Remembering You Comrade Bardhan first published in India in 2018

ISBN 978-93-5002-585-7

Published by
AAKAR BOOKS
28 E Pocket IV, Mayur Vihar Phase I
Delhi 110 091, India
aakarbooks@gmail.com
www.aakarbooks.com

Front Cover image by **Prof. Alf Gunvald Nilsen**
Back cover image from *Outlook India*, photo by **Jitender Gupta**
Inside images by **Vivek Sharma and others**
Designed by **Rajneesh Shrivastava**

Printed at
D.K. Fine Art Press, Delhi

CONTENT

Preface

LIFE OF A COMRADE

This is for the first time in last so many decades that Com. Bardhan is not with us in the Party Congress. Some of us have memories of Comrade Bardhan and personal anecdotes which we have tried to put down in words. We thought of sharing these views about Com. Bardhan with other comrades at this occasion of the Kollam Party Congress.

When he passed away on 2nd January, 2016, we were all very upset. It was Nandini Sundar who persuaded me to not just feel sad and to write about him. I wrote a piece in the form of a farewell letter which was published in the news platform *thewire.in*. He had a wide spectrum of friends and well wishers ranging from journalists and poets to labour leaders and politicians. Obviously many people wrote many memoirs and articles about him. It is difficult to be selective but it is also not possible to compile everything together.

He was the Chairperson of Joshi-Adhikari Institute of Social Studies and it was he who brought us into this institute so we thought it would be nice to bring out this publication from JAISS with brief write ups from S.P. Shukla and Jaya Mehta on Com. Bardhan.

Com. Bardhan didn't know me at all. It was because of Jaya and Shuklaji that I could get to know him and through him the Party and the Left.

S. P. Shukla is President of JAISS and it was also on Com. Bardhan's insistence that he agreed to be associated with the institute in this capacity. Com. Bardhan and Shuklaji used to enjoy each other's company a lot. And as Jaya put it, "it was a treat for us to listen to their conversation" whether it be on history, politics or any subject.

Jaya suggested that it would be nice if we include impressions of some comrades who used to meet him often and generally kept that feelings to their own heart.

Comrade Bardhan used to come every day, in the morning and in the evening to meet with the Red Guards, sat with them, read newspapers, some chit chat with whoever comes to meet him on the gate itself. In a way, Red Guards were his eyes and ears towards outside world. This practice has been there even when Com. Bardhan was a young comrade and Com. Rajeswara Rao or Com. Indrajeet Gupt were leading the party.

The Red Guards are senior comrades and have seen ups and downs of individuals and the party. Comrade Bardhan used to spend almost two hours of the day in the company of these comrades. We thought it would be nice to know how they think of Com. Bardhan? What are their impressions of a senior leader? Though, as mentioned, these Red Guard comrades are quite seasoned and politically mature, they don't open up easily. They spoke less, but affectionately. We know that our exercise did not succeed completely as we failed to capture their feelings in words. Sometimes they just speak with their eyes and it would be wrong to give meaning to their symbolic language by us. So we are putting here what they narrated in the context and leaving the rest on the readers to read what could not be written.

We could not document Comrade Kedar Nath Jha's comments, another Red Guard comrade who incidentally went for a long holiday and was not well enough to respond over telephone. In addition to the Red Guard Comrades, we planned some more interviews; one of them was of Comrade Biswaroop Adhikari of All India Peace and Solidarity Organisation (AIPSO) who used to spend 10-12 or sometime even more hours every day in the hospital where Com. Bardhan was admitted in coma. He was very shy and hesitant. He said, "What can I say about him. Many others know him better than me."

Similarly, I thought of collecting Dayaram's reminiscences as well, who used to take away the clothes from Ajoy Bhawan for ironing and washing. Two-three times, I witnessed their discussion and every time it was fun. He was certainly 15-20 years younger to Com. Bardhan but his health was not good. He had some problem in breathing. He used to breathe very fast. Com. Bardhan always used to tell him, "you have become very old. Now stop working." And he would respond by saying, "No, I am alright. You are old." Then they used to count ironing charges per cloth.

Com. Bardhan, "What! Rs. 10 per cloth for washing and ironing? Have you become crazy? This is too much."

And Dayaram would reply, "Do you know where the prices have gone? Even Rs. 10 is less but I am charging these discounted rates from you only."

He would tell him that he was being unfair. He would even say charging so heavily is no less than loot and extortion. At last, Com. Bardhan would count the clothes once more and he would pay more than what he settled on with the washerman, but he won't let Dayaram go without having an argument over the rates. I couldn't talk to Dayaram also as he has not been seen around Ajoy Bhawan for many months. Still, by mentioning these names here, I am registering their homage to Com. Bardhan.

We have gathered Com. Lallan's recollection of Com. Bardhan's memories. Com. Lallan has been driving the Party car since 2012.

We talked to Com. Bahadur. He used to take care of Com. Bardhan's medicines and food. He too shared his views very briefly.

While collecting these memories from comrades, I also revisited and relived those memorable moments full of life. In this way, we have brought him to Kollam Party Congress to get his best wishes to make it a success. Let us not believe that he is not with us. Let us believe that he is with us, in our hearts, in our works, on our fists and slogans, in our conviction to carry forward the legacy of the Party and the Red Flag.

Many among us definitely have a much longer association and many more things to remember. Perhaps this modest beginning will take us into a journey of the past where along with Comrade Bardhan, we can remember many of our senior comrades and draw inspiration to go ahead with our struggles to make this world a better place.

He was an excellent orator and exercised command over many languages. He was a voracious reader and a prolific writer. Two of his own articles are being reproduced here to give readers an idea about his grip on pen and also of his unflinching commitment for the party, ideology and the downtrodden.

Vineet Tiwari

HE LIVES IN COUNTLESS HEARTS

S.P. Shukla

Dear Com. Vineet,

You asked me to write a few words for the brochure you were preparing on Com Bardhan. I wondered what could I, a run-of-the-mill civil servant for most of my active life, say about someone who earned a place in the heart of countless colleagues, comrades and admirers. About someone who contributed handsomely to the making of modern India. About someone who unintentionally carved a place for himself in those annals. About someone who lived life of a true communist.

Com. Bardhan was only eight years older to me in age, but infinitely ahead of me in selfless public service and unflinching commitment to the cause of socialist transformation.

I had heard of him and also seen him much before I came in closer contact with him which began in the aftermath of the demolition of the Babri Masjid and all it signified. The friendship deepened as we shared many meetings and consultations in the context of India signing WTO in 1995. As part of the Indian Peoples' Campaign against WTO (with Late V.P Singh as its nucleus and inspiration), there were frequent opportunities for closer contact and sharing of views, not only on WTO but on many other issues and developments.

And soon, the acquaintance turned into comradeship.

He asked me to address a party workers' class on WTO and Intellectual Property issues. He was intently listening to me throughout. He got the text of my talk published. A little later he asked me to tell him all about patents. I wrote a small piece which prompted him to ask 'for more', to use his own words. He told me to write an expanded brochure with the title: "All About Patents". I started on it but could not progress much with other preoccupations intervening. I remember his words when he introduced me to one of his senior colleagues in the party whom I was seeing for the first time. He said "They will tell you about him as a bureaucrat and his work. That is fine. But for me he is a comrade first and last." His generosity was a tad too much, I said. But he said that is how he felt.

His generosity was not a momentary impulse. He genuinely valued others' views and assessments. His reactions too were frank and unvarnished. Although he was quite versed, when occasion so demanded, to deflect the query with a witty remark or a wry comment.

While I was living in Delhi, it was not unusual for him to suggest that I come along to Ajoy Bhavan to have a chat. And if I wished to see him, it was always an open door, a cup of hot coffee and warm reception. He never hedged his views and his comments on events and persons were unsparing. But he was more than generous in appreciating others' contributions.

That was 2004, when the first UPA was being formed with the support of the Left and a Common Minimum Programme was under discussion. I was away in Kumaon hills in Uttarakhand. Com Bardhan called me on phone and asked me to give my reaction to the draft of CMP. It was urgent and he was interested in my views, he added. I told him that I had not seen the text. Newspapers reached my place of residence the next day and the nearest working PC was in the branch office of SBI in a relatively bigger village located eight kms away from my place. The solution was found that he would Email the text to me C/o Branch Manager and I would drive down, access it there and send my comments right from there.

He did exactly that and I did my bit. It needs hardly to be added that my radical suggestions could not become part of the commonality!

But his concern for my views was etched on my memory.

Notwithstanding a measure of achievement in regard to National Rural Employment Guarantee Programme and modification of Land Acquisition Policy, politics were changing fast and for worse, particularly after 2009. The Left was not in a position to arrest the process, either in parliament or outside. The situation was crying out for a new, out-of-the-box initiative. Or so I thought.

It was the occasion of his 87th birthday on 25.09.12. I knew Com. Bardhan was far beyond the routine of birthday wishing. Nevertheless I decided to send him birthday greetings. And even more, I took the risk of suggesting to him some such initiative. Which many others in a similar position could have found uncalled for, if not cheeky. But not Com. Bardhan. He gave it a serious thought and wrote back promtply - a candid but positive reply. I can do no better than reproduce my communication to him, not so much to recall what I wrote or its relevance but to illustrate its openness, receptivity and generosity that characterised Com. Bardhan's respons to persons with little direct experience of the complexities of party politics.

25.09.12

Dear Comrade Bardhan,

I wish you a very happy birthday and a very long span of life, "Sharadah Shatam", as the saying goes. In your case such a wish cannot only be an expression of affectionate regards, which undoubtedly it is. A long life, of total dedication to revolutionary politics, of struggles, sacrifice and service creates its own 'field' of influence and expectations, extending far beyond the close circle of comrades, colleagues and associates, and, if I may add, the party. And it is that 'field' that inspires ordinary individuals like me to make bold to say what I intend to say in this birthday greeting.

It was almost a year ago that I wrote a piece in EPW, which, I believe, was brought to your notice and which, I have reason to feel, you had appreciated. I had said therein:

"We have two main entities on the political scene moving on their respective inexorable path like the heroes of the Greek Tragedy. Congress can not but continue the defence of the indefensible. And BJP must move on to become a Modi party"

"The geometry of political space is forcing the two major contestants on their respective inexorable trajectory. One is bound to get more and more embroiled in its own doings and get more and more discredited. The other who is dying to return to the position of power will be compelled by the logic of its trajectory to shed the mask of responsible democratic politics and reveal its majoritarian and anti-democratic stance overtly. In the process, both the formations are in the danger of losing some elements constituting its present support. As a result, a niche may open up for those political parties/groups/elements that are engaged in transformative politics. But it would not do if the relatively more important among them choose simply to repeat the erstwhile approach of opportunist electoral combines that have lost credibility over the last two decades. What is necessary is to build a broad, democratic platform which is radical in its agenda and non-sectarian in its approach. Only such a political initiative will have the potential of carrying forward the process of democratization of the polity and confronting effectively the triple challenge of the agrarian crisis, the alienation of the minorities and the territorially peripheral states, and the burgeoning threat to democratic rights and freedoms."

I ended the piece saying "In short, the churning that the last year has produced has disturbed the placidity of the political scene. It has opened up political possibilities. A chance for transformative politics has emerged better than only a year ago. But if those engaged in such politics fail to seize the initiative, remain content with their isolated, sectarian struggles and leave the big picture to its own dynamics, the possibility of politics getting more turbid and moving in the direction of more authoritarian and non-democratic tendencies, not only of the BJP variety, can not be ruled out".

If anything, developments during the year that followed have only vindicated the analysis. By the same token, they have deepened the apprehensions: and dialectically, opened up new political possibilities.

In the past (1989, 1996), the Left had lent its support to a centrist political grouping to defeat the corrupt/reactionary forces from continuing/seizing power. But both the experiments were short-lived and, ultimately ended lending credibility to either of the mainstream political formations, first the Congress and, later, the BJP. The Left's tactical support to Congress in 2004 not only defeated the threat of the return of BJP to power but also brought the left in a greater national focus and in a far more favourable light. But the experiment ended adversely for the left, despite its principled opposition on the nuclear issue, for the reasons which need not detain us here. Two aspects, however, must be underlined: the left was betrayed by its important ally viz. SP and the Congress did not blink in executing most unscrupulous and undemocratic manoeuvres in dealing with the opposition.

The situation today is qualitatively quite different. There is no reliable, charismatic nucleus around which a left of the centre coalition could be forged in terms of an electoral combine. The erstwhile components of such a combine in the past have either betrayed the trust, or have been discredited or simply do not have significant presence. The Congress has repeatedly shown that it is irrevocably wedded to neo-liberal agenda and there is no hope whatsoever of it reverting to its centrist, leave alone mildly progressive, politics. Any move of direct or indirect, active or passive association with these forces will only discredit the left forces and further weaken their political role.

A political vacuum is being generated by the total loss of credibility of the binary political process represented by UPA and NDA, on the one hand, and the rank opportunism of the so-called regional political outfits, on the other. The vacuum is attracting apparently apolitical Ramdevs and Annas and VK Singhs to the forefront of political scene as "saviours". It is also giving rise to infantile politics like that of Arvind Kejriwal. The net result of these developments will only favour the re-emergence of the binary politics of Congress and BJP in the medium run, leaving the transformative, people-centric politics on the margins of the political power.

The historic role of the mainstream Left is to fill this vacuum legitimately and save the polity from the perpetuation of increasingly anti-democratic neo-liberal politics of the binary forces or the eventual descent of the Indian polity into communal/fascist/anarchist politics of disintegration. To that end, the Left has to cast its net too wide, move away from its latent or manifest sectarianism, go beyond its close-knit cadre based politics, transform itself into a mass political formation and become a vanguard of a broad democratic front. I can see that this may amount to asking for the moon.

How do we bridge this gap between the historic role that is demanded of the Left and its constituent character? The answer perhaps lies in a veteran of the left like you taking the lead in transcending the mainstream left. I am speaking of transcending, not parting with, the left.

For the last two years, some of us have been working together to mobilize support for a radical and inclusive political platform on the basis of a set of clearly formulated policy objectives. We have recognized that an important political imperative of such an initiative has to be that it is left-friendly, although it is not a constituent of the Left as such. While the framework paper that we have adopted analyses the political situation in the country, we have steered clear of sophisticated ideological debates in our presentation and concentrated on the policy objectives, which are naturally convergent, if not coincident, with the major thrust of the left political programme. We felt that that kind of an approach will provide flexibility to muster wider support for a broad democratic front.

It may turn out to be a priceless return birthday gift from you to all of us, if you give a serious thought to what we are seeking to do and share with us your reaction/critique .

With all the best wishes and warm regards,

S.P.SHUKLA

COMMUNIST PARTY OF INDIA

Central Office

Ajoy Bhavan, 15, Com. Indrajit Gupta Marg, New Delhi-110002
Telephone: 23232801, 23235058, Fax: 23235543, Email: cpiofindia@gmail.com

Secretary: A.B.Bardhan

New Delhi
Dated : 27th September 2012

Dear Com. Shuklaji,

Thank you for your warm message of greetings. Getting old is by itself no achievement. The only thing that one can wish for at this age is to keep on working for the cause till the end.

You have imposed a huge burden on me. I don't know if I am worthy of it or capable of bearing it.

I have read through the note that you have written. It is as good and exciting as your well-known article in the EPW. I fully agree with you. I cannot yet say whether the Left can breakout of its sectarian self-isolation. To some extent we are prisoners of our own 'politics and our own shell'. But let us try. The situation demands it.

I am expecting your comment on the Party Programme.

With warm regards and best wishes.

Yours
A.B.Bardhan
(A.B.Bardhan)

To
Shri S.P. Shukla
B-35, Forest Frails
Survey No. 16 & others
Near Manas Lake, Mauje Bhugaon
Pune – 412 115 (Maharashtra)

In November 2015, Com. Bardhan suggested a symposium be organised on "Communal Fascism and Growing Intolerance" in December 2015. I responded that perhaps it could be slated for January or February 2016 as a similar event was organised in Delhi only weeks ago and we would let some gap to intervene which would also give us a longer time for preparation. He considered the argument and came back reiterating that symposium be held in December 2015 only. We respected his decision. The symposium was organised on 02.12.15. He chaired it throughout. He did not speak much but his interest and concentration was as alert as ever.

The very next day, he called a special meeting to consider the question of fund-raising for JAISS. Without any fuss, he started the meeting with the quiet statement of his personal donation of Rs. One lakh. There was no better way of tackling the agenda upfront. That was Com. Bardhan's way.

As the future unfolded, those two events turned out to be his last public events.

In retrospect, we realised with anguish why he insisted on an early date in December 2015 rather than one in February 2016 as we had suggested. He ended his journey on 2nd January 2016. Now in April 2018, we are witnessing much greater turmoil, much darker times.

The need for an out-of-the-box political initiative seems more pressing than ever. The case for a radical and inclusive political platform looks all the more imperative.

Remembering Com. Bardhan should stir us into thinking a new and confronting political agenda upfront.

The window of opportunity for such an initiative may also not last too long.

SP Shukla is the President of Joshi-Adhikari Institute of Social Studies and Centre for Policy Analysis (CPA), New Delhi. He has served as the Finance Secretary of India and as a member of the Planning Commission.

I LEARNT A LOT FROM YOU

Jaya Mehta

One does not require an occasion to remember Comrade Bardhan. We remember him all the time. If you reach Ajoy Bhawan in the morning and go to the second floor, he would be sitting in office secretary's room reading newspapers. If you go to the canteen at lunch time, he would be sitting at last bench on the right side, where a patch of sun would be waiting for him. When he sat there, comrades would surround him. He would be listening to them and talking. He would eat very little - one or perhaps two hot chapatis and some vegetable.

If clouds came suddenly and it started raining he would come down and sit on the steps at the entrance. You could persuade him to have tea. And in the evening when people were going back home, he would be sitting outside with the red guards or sometimes with other comrades. All current political gossip and happenings were talked about. No one ever felt that one was talking to the general secretary – a big leader who commanded great respect from every quarter.

Sometimes, comrade would come and sit in our room. He would tell us stories of his young days, of other leaders or stories from Russian history. He read a lot. There were always books on his table which Vineet borrowed. He would go through a book or an article very quickly and give his opinion. And then one would be surprised at the details that he had assimilated in his quick reading. He wrote also effortlessly. His command over language was very good and expression very precise.

I and Vineet joined Joshi Adhikari Institute because Shuklaji talked to Com. Bardhan and asked him to include us in the research activities of the party. In fact we came to know Comrade through

Shuklaji. When Shuklaji came to Ajoy Bhawan to meet him and the two sat together. It was a treat for us. Comrade really was very fond of Shuklaji and respected him a great deal. The two would talk for long time. The warmth and rapport between them was like they were old friends. Shuklaji often told Comrade, 'let us go round the country and only you can persuade all the left forces to join together and become a force in the political scene.' It is sad that the project could not be accomplished.

I personally learnt a lot from Comrade.

Our research project in Joshi Adhikari Institute was a survey of marginal and small farmers across the country. We had invited Kisan Sabha comrades to help with the survey. Comrade Bardhan came to address the first meeting. He said to Kisan Sabha activists, 'I am glad you are doing this project. After Hare Krishna Konar and Binoy Chowdhury, we comrades have given up the habit of listening to people. We are so busy telling them our point of view, we never have time to find out how people are living and what they are thinking.'

After we published the report, I learnt that some comrades made some adverse comments. I was very upset. Comrade said to me, 'people are different, they think differently. You cannot get so emotional if someone does not appreciate your work. But do not lose confidence in your findings and your inferences.'

During Comrade Bardhan's tenure as general secretary, party's electoral performance went down hill. I learnt from Comrade how to face defeat gracefully and not lose confidence in you conviction. I learnt from him how to appreciate adversaries and their work.

I had studied German Democratic Republic society and economy in detail. I spent 3 months in Berlin visiting GDR's Hoch Schule i.e. their Planning Commission. I was very impressed with the socialist society of GDR. Again I spent one month in Berlin at the time of German unification. I witnessed how the socialist society was vilified and demolished by the powerful western propaganda and politics. I went to Berlin again in 2013. I met my old friends there. I was thinking that my friends from the university will be remembering the advantages that socialist society offered to weaker sections – the women, children and old people. I came back very disappointed. In 2013, I could not meet any one who had fond memories of socialist GDR. No one thought of any advantages that socialist society offered. When I came back I shared my disappointment with Comrade Bardhan. He first heard me with great patience, then smiled and said, 'You went back to that country after 23 years and you were expecting the society as you left in 1990. Things don't remain in stasis, they change and people also change.'

Shuklaji coined a phrase 'inclusive but radical.' I saw Comrade Bardhan living that kind of life – politically and personally. Red Salute to Comrade. You are there with us to guide us in these difficult times and to give us strength.

Dr. Jaya Mehta is a senior economist working full time with Joshi-Adhikari Institute since 2009. She was earlier associated with Gokhale Institute of Politics and Economics, Pune, Indian Institute of Advance Studies, Shimla and Nehru Memorial Museum and Library, New Delhi.

A FAREWELL LETTER TO A.B. BARDHAN

Vineet Tiwari

Dear Comrade Bardhan,

To write someone's obituary, one needs to believe that person is no more. With all due regard to materialism, I am not willing to accept that you have gone. It is true that you are not there to answer our questions anymore and it is also true that I can no longer offer you homemade *laddus* made by my mother, which you used to like very much. While going upstairs, after taking a walk in the Ajoy Bhawan yard, you won't knock my door and say *"Haan bhai?"* (what's up?). Despite all this, I feel that you are still around.

So, because you have done something new by bidding goodbye to your physical presence, I will also add something new to our relations. I have never written a letter to you, so I am writing one now.

I want to start by telling you some funny things. I collected several condolence messages, which appeared after the rumour of your death spread on December 7, 2015. I was looking forward to laughing over them with you, and discussing the hurried character of social media, where instant reactions are more important than substance.

On January 2, 2016, your son Ashok, Com. Adhikari, your caretaker Kanhaiya and I were standing outside the ICU Ward no. 6 of G. B Pant Hospital's Neurology Department. Somebody told us that the news of Com. Bardhan's death was being broadcast on Malayalam TV Channels. I immediately called a journalist in one of these channels, a friend of mine, and told him I was at the hospital and no such thing had happened. I scolded him for not checking the facts, before putting them on air. In the meantime, Ashok was called inside the ICU by the doctor and told that you had passed away.

When Ashok told me, I first wondered how the media had known of your death, even before us. The answer was obvious: some hospital staff member had thought it more important to inform the media, than tell the family.

When living, your engagement with the media was very different. You were friendly to young journalists and laughed with them, but would refuse to give them a bite if you thought the issue was not of real importance. You were polite, but also stubborn. When I first moved to Ajoy Bhawan in 2010, we hardly knew each other. But I saw you dealing with intellectuals, with common people and with comrades from various quarters. Perhaps you were harsh at times, but you always listened. As Shabnam Hashmi said, you were the most easily accessible leader.

ACCESSIBLE, EVEN ACROSS PARTY LINES

I remember when some comrades came from Madhya Pradesh when you were resting in your room. You welcomed them. There were never any qualms; and no one felt the need to take a prior appointment. When Soni Sori and Linga from Chhattisgarh (who later joined the Aam Admi Party) came to Ajoy Bhawan, I took them to your room, where D. Raja and Annie also joined us. You heard their sufferings and asked Raja to write a letter to the then Prime Minister, Manmohan Singh. Another morning, a few years ago, I was surprised to see you in Ajoy Bhawan before 10 am. This was a time when you stayed in a flat with Sudhakar Reddy. When I asked you, *"Comrade, how come you are here this early?,"* you replied, *"Do you know where I am coming from?"* Seeing that I was clueless, you said, *"Chidambaram, I went to meet P. Chidambaram regarding some medical requirements of Kobad Ghandy (of the CPI Maoist) as he is ill in jail."*

When we showed you photographs of women standing in water and doing *jalsatyagrah* in Khandwa district of Madhya Pradesh, I

The sum total of A.B. Bardhan's possessions, after a life spent in politics: A rusted almirah with some clothes, a pair of shoes and this red travel suitcase, which he used for the past five years.

Credit: Bhupinder

remember the pain which appeared on your face. You immediately wanted to do something. My decision to become a party member was less the result of my knowledge of Marxist theory and more because I observed you construct a life based on that theory.

OPEN BUT PRINCIPLED

When the 2014 Lok Sabha election result was about to be declared, someone circulated an article accusing you and Abhay Sahu in Odisha of trying to weaken the anti- POSCO movement, because of the CPI's interest in allying with the Biju Janata Dal. I informed you about the mail in circulation, and asked you hesitatingly, *"Comrade, is it true? That we allowed the struggle to weaken so that some seats could be negotiated with the BJD?"* You responded with your usual firmness, *"What rubbish. We contest elections and we make alliances but that doesn't mean that anybody can ask us to change our politics."* The alliance eventually did not take place.

You remembered thousands of comrades by name, you did not follow bureaucratic channels of functioning, and you did not hesitate to break or cross lines if it was to help others.When Jaya Mehta read that 14 Musahars had been given a life sentence in the Amousi carnage case (in which 16 Kurmis were killed in 2009), she talked to you and said that it should be investigated. She had the feeling that the Amousi case, which was projected as a caste issue, actually involved a land conflict. After listening to her calmly, you called Badri Narayan Lal who was then Bihar secretary and asked for an update on the Amousi case. Since Amousi is in Khagaria district, he said he would get back to you after discussing this with Satyanarayan Singh, who is from Khagaria. Without waiting for him, you directly called Satyanarayan Singh and asked him to help investigate the Amousi case. The very next day after the Patna party congress, we left for Amousi. It was one of the most difficult terrains we had ever seen. The report we wrote, thanks to your support, perhaps contributed towards the eventual acquittal of the accused.

NEVER DESPONDENT

You surprised me after the Bihar assembly election results in 2015. Again, it was Jaya who suggested that comrades from other states should help campaign for Left candidates. You immediately endorsed the idea but added, *"your presence should not burden the local party."* You were actively involved in the election plan but when the results were declared, and I phoned you from Indore, you were not sad. You just said, *"We need to do more work. Ladenge, koi baat nahi."* (We shall fight, don't get disheartened.)

Simplicity, straight forwardness, compassion, warmth and welcoming behaviour – you were an amalgamation of all these human qualities. But what made you different was the capacity to foresee the times ahead and the ability to open yourself to new options with a left perspective.

S. P. Shukla was very keen that you start learning the internet, and asked me to teach you. One day, you called me to your room and brought a small laptop out of the drawer of your table. You told me it had been lying there unused since your son Ashok bought it. I was surprised to see how fast you started learning. The only problem was that you were afraid of making some mistake, which would spoil the computer. And my many reassurances didn't work in this regard. Unfortunately, our traveling schedules didn't allow us to continue further with this exercise.

UNASSUMING

One day, Shuklaji insisted that you should write about yourself. You refused, saying, *"Autobiographies are always biased. What I think about issues concerning society is clear from my writings and what I think about people is not important for people to know since it is subjective. People who have written about me have ascribed good or bad qualities that I did not know I possessed."*

This also reminds me of your dialogue with Jaya one evening in Ajoy Bhawan, when she was leaving for Amsterdam to address an

international meeting. Jaya was nervous and feeling unprepared to take a six hour session with international students. You said *"Hey, why are you going there? Our Praful (Bidwai) died there, you know."* Then you calmed Jaya by sharing your own experience, *"You know one thing. I also feel nervous many times when I have to speak. But it is only for the first 2-3 minutes, then the words flow automatically."*

I remember when I had a problem regarding my organisation, the Progressive Writers' Association (PWA). It was troubling me emotionally, and I was almost on the verge of crying. Jaya took me to you and asked you to give me direction. I told you about my dilemma – having to accept the resignation of a senior writer who had brought me into the PWA. You heard me peacefully without saying anything. Then you came to my room in the evening and started in your usual style, *"You know one thing?"* And then you described how you joined the party after being inspired by stories of S.A. Dange, but when the party decided to take action against him, it was you and Homi Daji who sat together, in this very room, here where this bed is kept, and drafted the resolution. I overcame my emotions and did what was needed for the organisation.

WORKING TILL THE END

On November 28-29, 2015 you attended a two-day seminar of Asian communist party delegates on the occasion of 90 years of the CPI. But what you were most keen on was a symposium on communal fascism and intolerance, which was held on December 2, 2015. You were there from 9 in the morning to 7 in the evening and even later, you talked a lot about the future plans of the Joshi-Adhikari Institute of Social Studies with S. P. Shukla who came all the way from Pune on your insistence. That was the last time people saw you in public.

I came to your room to bid you goodbye on December 5, 2015. I told you that I was going to Govind Pansare's house to interview Uma Pansare, Smita, Megha and other comrades; you held my hand with your firm grip and without saying anything in words, gave me a reassuring look. I remember you saying that you had lost many people in this long life of nine decades but never cried as much as you did after hearing about the murder of Com. Pansare. He was very dear to you. I left on the 5th and got the news of your stroke on the 7th. I was sure of giving you a book on Pansare in the New Year as a gift. Your return gift would have been to read the book.

SHARING REMINISCENCES

We saw the entire film *Fall of Berlin* on a laptop together with a young journalist, Sachin. I remember very vividly how you became nostalgic when Stalin appeared in the film and gave his famous speech celebrating victory over fascism. You asked us to pause the movie and told us that you heard that speech along with other comrades on radio in Nagpur. You watched that entire movie with a lot of interest but when it was over, you made a characteristic ice-cold comment. *"It was a propaganda film and not a very artistic one."*

Later, on the occasion of your fast against corruption at Jantar Mantar, where JNU IPTA sang some revolutionary songs, you told me that you used to sing when you were 14-15 years old. Along with a friend, you sang to attract people to public meetings. After some persuasion, you sang us a few lines of a Baul song in Ajoy Bhawan. I think this is the reason you remained interested in cultural activities till the end. Coincidentally, when I took a photographer to your room, I found the latest issue of *Vasudha* (the literary magazine of the MP Progressive Writers' Association) lying on the table.

You told us stories about your underground activities. You told us about how you remembered your mother's courage when travelling in a boat on the Ganges, which was about to sink in a thunderstorm. You narrated how you were groomed in politics: *"I used to go to various political meetings with a senior leader famous for his speeches. He made jokes and the audience would applaud. I also used to speak but my speeches were not that effective. I thought maybe I should also make some*

A.B. Bardhan and his wife, Padma

jokes in my speech. So I went and told jokes to the audience. It had no effect. I thought perhaps the audience was in no mood for jokes. However, when my leader made a speech and told jokes, they applauded. I felt very frustrated. Then my leader called me and told me in Marathi, 'You spoke well, but why copy? Make your own style.' I understood then, people want the original, not a copy."

Once when you were sitting in this room where I am writing, you informed me that this was the same room where Gangadhar Adhikari, Romesh Chandra, Kaifi Azmi, Homi Daji and many others had stayed. I responded saying I had heard about this from other comrades, and all of them including Lenin whose bust is in front of my room, knock at my door at night and we discuss various issues. You laughed heartily.

OUR CONVERSATIONS WILL CONTINUE

On January 4, 2016, we bid you goodbye at the Nigambodh Ghat crematorium. I opened my door many times that night to see your photograph placed near Lenin's bust. You and I were alone in the corridor of Ajoy Bhawan. I got the feeling that even though you lived over 90 years, your departure was far too soon for me. After a certain age, it is very difficult to make new friends, and you were one of my closest and most sensible friends. We had many unfinished discussions on China, Vietnam, Nepal, worker-peasant alliances, cooperatives, strengthening the party, etc and I feel at a loss. I know that no one remains forever. But people like you live on through their ideas. In the coming nights, I know you will join my discussions with Lenin, Romesh Chandra and all the others, and I will offer you kettle made coffee again.

I wanted to show you a photograph of yours taken on 2nd December, 2016, but you didn't allow me to do that. In the photo, your magnetic smiling shining eyes are very beautiful. This is a beauty one only gets if you dream of a bright future and have a clear understanding of the past. This beauty has to be earned.

Lal Salaam, Com. Bardhan. You will remain with us. I hope your presence will bring out something good in all of us for the betterment of the Party and for the cause of socialism.

Your chum (as you called me once),

Vineet

(Published in 'The Wire' on 12th January 2016)

Vineet Tiwari is a political and cultural activist, journalist and poet. He is associated with Joshi-Adhikari Institute of Social Studies since 2009. He is the National Secretary of Progressive Writers' Association (PWA) and National Executive Member of Indian Peoples' Theatre Association (IPTA).

Com. A.B. Bardhan and Com. Govind Pansare

OUR PARTY - THE CPI

A.B. Bardhan

Seventy years in the life of a party is long enough to judge the sort of the party it is, and to assess its contribution to the country's political social life.

The CPI was born in the course of the country's fight against alien rule, and under the impact of the great October revolution which illumined a new path for all oppressed people. It grew through the militant and class upsurge of the workers, the struggles of the peasants and students manifested in a wave of strikes, anti-landlord actions, anti-imperialist boycotts and *hartals*.

It arose out of the fusion of militant patriotism and internationalism, of the struggle for national liberation and the class struggle for socialism.

The party became the confluence of several streams of revolutionary freedom- fighters who cheerfully embraced martyrdom, faced long imprisonment and tortures, and were drawn towards the ideology of Marxism and inspired by the noble goal of socialism.

They rededicated themselves to the task of organizing the working class and other toiling sections in their mass and class organizations, so that they could fight for a better life and democratic rights, and imbibe class consciousness through the school of such struggles.

The party went among the most deprived and downtrodden, the wretched of the earth, and raised among them the banner of social emancipation. It has from birth made its voice heard against all forms of exploitation and social oppression, for equality and social justice.

Several thousands of its cadres and ranks have fallen victims to the bullets and *lathis* of the police, the hired assassins of landlords and capitalists while upholding the rights of the people. It is a party of martyrs, of sacrifices, of trials and tribulations, but all for the cause.

It is the party that first called for the overthrow of British imperialist rule for India's complete independence, years before the congress adopted it as its demand in 1929.

It is the party that first came forward with a comprehensive programme of the anti- imperialist and democratic revolution, a programme which gave content to our vision of a Free India, much before the congress formally adopted several elements of it as its Karachi session in 1931. Included in the programme were the demands for:

Land to the tiller!
Nationalization of foreign capital!
Adult suffrage!
Nation's wealth in the nation's hands!
Eight hour working day!
Democratic rights of organization, meeting demonstration and strike!
Social equality for women!
Social justice for the untouchables!

But we do not live in the past only, basking in our glory, recalling the history of all past struggles and their legendary heroes. There have been many parties which started with great revolutionary promise, but later could not live up to it. We have occasionally strayed from the path, deviated to the right or to the left, committed serious mistakes and paid dearly for them.

But soon we have been back on the correct revolutionary path. We are a party of the contemporary epoch, and a party of the future. That is attested to by our firm belief in the ideology of Marxism-Leninism, our unshakeable faith in socialism, in our constant struggle for our country's future and our people's interests.

After freedom, we have further developed and enriched our programme and our activities with a view to complete the democratic revolution and go forward to a just socialist society, which will end all forms of exploitation based on caste, class and gender, a society in which wealth produced by the toiling millions will not be appropriated by a few.

The struggle today has become more bitter, more intense, and more complex, and the party is unrelentingly engaged in this struggle.

Imperialism is using new instruments like the IMF, the World Bank, the newly spawned World Trade Organization and the MNCs, and new forms such as the structural adjustments programme to dominate and exploit the Third World countries, including India.

It is in this context that the party opposes and fights the new economic policies, for they weaken and destroy our public sector, erode our self- reliance, allow MNCs to acquire control over indigenous industries, push our country into a debt trap, intensify social tensions, and further aggravate the problems of poverty, unemployment, illiteracy and disease. The party has consistently and at all times fought against all communal and divisive forces, against all types of fundamentalism—be it of majority or minority variety—it believes in the unity and integrity of the country, in the brotherhood of our people irrespective of their militant class unity against forces of reaction that seek to divide and rule over them.

Communists have tried to intervene wherever possible to prevent riots. To protect the lives and properties of innocent people especially the minorities who are targeted in such riots. For this they have sometimes paid with their lives. They have worked hard to provide relief and rehabilitation to the affected people during all such and other calamities.

In the Punjab, the party bravely opposed the Khalistani terrorists with the defiant slogan: *"Na Hindu Raj, Na Khalistan: Jug Jug Jive Hindustan!"* More than 100 communists laid down their lives in this struggle.

In the present context when the *Sangh Parivar* roused communal frenzy, targeted the *Babri Masjid* for destruction, communists were in the forefront in the campaign against the communal forces who have been emboldened by the recent supreme court judgment.

The party has always upheld values and probity in public life, and therefore exposed corruption at high levels, the nexus between money power and muscle power, the nexus between bourgeois politicians, bureaucrats and the police. It fights all this, for without that there can be no democracy, no socialism.

The party recognizes and is proud of our rich cultural heritage, the variety and beauty of its folk culture; it realizes the importance of culture in our people's life. It therefore took the initiative to take culture to our people by helping in setting up the Indian People Theatre's Association and in setting up the Progressive Writers Association.

Today, when our cultural pluralism is threatened and neo-fascist obscurantism is seeking to take over, helped by imperialist cosmopolitanism and consumerism, the party stresses this task all the more.

Saluting the rising new generation, the youth of our country, the party gives priority to the struggle for education and employment under the slogan: *"Education for all, Jobs for all"*. We are a party which knows it has no interests higher or different from the working people, the country.

We are proud that it is our party that spread the message of socialism and brought hope of a bright tomorrow for our ancient and long-suffering land and its multi-crore people.

Today, when we have to defeat the Congress and the BJP and put forward a third alternative before our people, a left, democratic and secular alternative, the party consistently strives for the unity of the left forces in our country.

The split has damaged the communist movement, but to overcome the consequences and to defeat the Congress and the BJP, the party stands for communist unity on a principled basis, for left unity on the basis of shared ideals, for left and democratic unity on the basis of a common minimum programme.

In pursuit of our goal during the last 70 years, we have made important contributions, and influenced the country's politics and its destiny. Our struggles and sacrifices have not been in vain. Without our party, the mass organizations would have been weaker, poorer and directionless. But we shall overcome!

There is no shortcut, no easy way to the goal. We do not look for short term gains, because short term gains obtained at the cost of principles only pave the way for heavy losses at the end.

We have withstood reverses and disappointments. The collapse of Soviet Union was a heavy blow. But we have been able to put all that behind us. Our patriotism has been rewarded. Those who crowd with delight, talking about the end of socialism and the death of Marxism, are now red in the face with embarrassment. They have been proved wrong.

On this 70th anniversary, let us vow to build a stronger party, close to the masses, strong in determination, firm in ideological commitment, sensitive to changes, and mature in applying Marxism to our specific conditions.

THE TRIBAL COMMUNITIES AND THE DEVELOPMENTAL EXPERIENCE

A.B. Bardhan

In the early 1950s Jawaharlal Nehru, who was remarkably active to the needs and aspirations of the tribal communities, had laid down the following principles for tribal development:

"The tribal people should develop along the lines of their own genius.....(We should) encourage in every way their own traditional arts and culture.....The tribal rights in land and forests should be respected.... (We should) train and build their own people to do the works of administration and development.....(We should) avoid introducing too many outsiders into the territory.....We should not over-administer their areas....We should work through and not in rivalry to, their social cultural institutions."

Past experience shows that every one of these principles, that has been termed as the 'panchasheela of tribal development' has been violated in practice.

Do they continue to be valid today? They do.

The tribal communities are by and large the victims of neglect. There is a lack of comprehension about their problems, about their criticality. In a country, where they constitute 7 percent of the population spread right across its waist and contemplated in certain economically and politically strategic areas , this has serious consequences.

The geography of hunger, illiteracy, extremely low level of economic development and political stagnation in the country coincides with the geography of the tribal people's homeland. Coincidentally this is the fate of indigenous population all over the world. After being virtually wiped off the face of African continents by the Spanish conquistadors and the immigrants who came in the wake of Columbus' discovery of America, and from the Australian continent by the wave of British felons who emigrated there, those who managed to survive have been severely marginalized by the white man's civilizing mission.

One can draw a little wry satisfaction from the fact that only now, a bit of international recognition has been accorded to the struggle of indigenous people against genocide and for their human and cultural rights by the award of the Nobel peace prize to the 30 year old Guatemalan Indian- American activist Rigoberta Menchu.

This is the golden jubilee year of the 'Quit India' movement, which heralded the last act of our freedom struggle. History has tended to ignore the role that the tribal people have played in the fight against the alien rulers.

Their struggles have been looked upon as so many isolated episodes, and leaders thrown up by them in the course of these struggles are revered only as folk heroes.

Actually the Kol insurrection , the Santhal Revolt headed by brother Kanu-Sidhu, the Bhil resistance, the armed struggle led by the legendary Birsa Munda, the Bastar rising, the Koya uprising under the intrepid leadership of Alluri Sitarama Raju, right down to the non-violent resistance of the Tana Bhagats, are a few in that series of struggles against the alien rulers of their camp followers which the tribal people had carried on, when others had for a time withdrawn from the battlefield after the failure of the first war of independence.

Along with other sections of our people, the tribal communities also looked forward to a new dawn of progress and development after freedom. But the mainstream of development has passed them by.

Indeed, it would be no exaggeration to say that the tribal communities have been the victims of the existing development process rather than its beneficiaries. Their dreams lie shattered.

It would be wrong of course, to lump together all tribal communities and regard them at the same stage on the scale of progress and development. There is inevitably a great deal of unevenness.

The communities in the north- east have a greater degree of illiteracy and unawareness of their rights as compared to the communities in the central and other regions, where we can still find them in a primitive or semi-primitive stage.

Democratic awareness and consciousness of identity, which motivate any ethnic community to voice its needs and aspirations, reach each community at different points of time. But by now, almost all tribal communities have started raising their voice, and solutions have to be found to their aspiration for development and progress.

What has been the effect of development al process so far on the tribals?

Without going too far into history, one notes that British overlordship had brought with it the mahajan, the sahukar, the fouzedar into tribal regions. These have been the traditional exploiters of the tribal communities

Indebtedness and bonded labour, exploitation by the mechanism of the market, cheated the tribals out of their lands. Private land ownership was something alien to the tribals who had community- managed land and common utilization.

In fact, this is a characteristic not only of the tribal communities in India, but of indigenous people all over the world. This natural bond was vividly expressed in the declaration which was adopted in the 1975 at the Conference of the indigenous people of the world at Aberny in Canada, which lamented poignantly that "other people stole their land from them, and them from their land".

The tribals were steadily displaced, pushed further and further to infertile, rocky and hilly tracts, uprooted from their lands deprived from their forests and scattered in inhospitable corners.

There took place large scale migration of Adivasis as an indentured and bonded labours, as plantation workers and collies, while 'outsiders' moved in, resulting in big demographic and socio-economic changes in traditional tribal areas.

The advent of freedom did little to reverse this process, despite some well meaning but half hearted legislations prohibiting alienation of Adivasis lands.

Rather the process of the alienations of Adivasis from land has been accelerated manifold because of several projects, private, and public, coming up precisely in tribal regions which happen to be rich in natural resources. Adivasis villages and lands cultivated by them through several generations together with adjoining forests were just taken away wholesale, officially 'acquired'.

Tens of thousands were deprived of their livelihood, to make way for projects, the symbols of modern development. In return they have got nothing except a few pieces of silver and casual employment for a few of them in the most unskilled jobs

They have no share in the huge National assets that have been built up during four decades of development largely at their expense. They have not shared in the prosperity. The transformation in their case is not even from the poor peasant cultivator to skilled industrial workers.

They have been cast aside to swell the ranks of landless labour, domestic labourer, destitute, casual and contract workers. The few pieces of silver some of them got as 'compensation' soon melted away for the tribals are not used to the wiles and guiles of commerce.

They have soon found themselves without steady means of sustenance and livelihood. There are exceptions here too, as anywhere else but such exceptions prove the rule.

The spread of industrialisation and Commerce have had a shattering effect on the life of the tribals. The class differentiation which these have brought about amongst other sections of the people, have not had the same impact on the tribals, whose culture and community life are based on different values.

One can at most say, that a small and scattered middle class has emerged among them, more because of the policy of reservation, even though in their case it is always far from being fulfilled. But this middle class is acquiring the strength to lead the whole community and voice its aspiration and demands.

Of late because of hue and cry, there is talk of 're-settling' the displaced tribals and other project affected on alternate lands. Invariably, these settlement offers are far away from the original place, or located upstream (if it is a dam or a canal), so that no water reaches the wretched plots of these people.

A lot is heard about the Narmada project. One may have different views about several aspects of this projects, its effect on the environment and so on. But can there be two opinions about the fate of tens of thousands tribal families whose homes and fields will be submerged, and the totally callous and inadequate 'official' schemes of resettlement planned for them?

Today they are reduced to the status of wage slaves for unscrupulous forest contractors, and the bonded labour of corrupt forest officials. Development and Commerce has advanced by ruthlessly plundering the forest wealth, by offering it up as a sacrifice at the altar of big money.

It is claimed that one crore and 50 lakh hectares, or 22 percent of our territory, is under forest. Actually not more than 12 % is under tree cover, whereas a vast country like ours should have at least 30 % under tree cover, for a correct ecological balance.

These days huge amount are being spent on afforestation and social forestry. But for this reliance is placed on the bureaucracy and not on the forest friendly adivasis. The results are naturally not commensurate with the funds spent and the aimed objectives. Even the trees are planted with an eye to their commercial use, and in most cases alien to the tribal living.

Afforestation can only be successfully undertaken by seeking the cooperation of the tribal people and other sections of rural masses encouraging them and rendering all possible help for growing a suitable mix of trees, which can supply the needs of fruits, fuel and other forest products and also enable them to market these at suitable prices. The tribals will themselves be the willing protectors of such forests.

Despite declarations about 'Garibi hatao' and Adivasi welfare in the 20 point programmes, tribal indebtedness is growing. Rising prices, chronic unemployment and underemployment, meager and irregular coverage of the public distribution system and its further curtailment, all these are further thrusting them deeper into indebtedness.

There is no stable Credit System which caters to their productive and consumer needs. The tribal is not credit worthy in the eyes of the banks. The tribal cooperative societies are mostly hotbeds of middlemen (mostly non-tribal) and many of the forest produce marketing coops have become tools for swindling the tribals of their dues.

A good deal of benefits conferred through tribal blocks and disintegrated tribal development projects have been reaped by non tribals living in those areas, since these are mostly manned by the bureaucratic- administrative set up and not through their own personal and social Institutions.

India's record in the spread of Mass education and eradication of illiteracy as a necessary vehicle of all round development, after more than four decades of freedom, is dismal. Even here the overall percentage figures hide the reality that literacy and education among Adivasis is much lower, except where the missionaries have played some role.

The percentage of 'drop outs' among Adivasi boys and girls is exceptionally high. Those who manage to reach secondary school and college standards are few.

This is one of the factors for the shortfall in the reservation quota meant for them and higher Institution and din jobs. It has prevented a qualified and sufficiently large personnel developing from among them.

RED GUARDS AND OTHER COMRADES

Inaugurated in 1969, Ajoy Bhawan has a unique architecture. It is a beautiful building which is plastered from outside by crushed small pieces of stone. It doesn't need paint from outside and stays ever young naturally. I was impressed by the design and elevation of the building so I did some research and found out some wonderful information. I got to know that Ajoy Bhawan was designed by one of the most notable architects of India, Cyrus Jhabvala. Learning more about him made me feel happier. I got to know that Cyrus Jhabvala was married to Ruth Pravar Jhabvala who is the only person so far who has received both Booker Award for her writings and two time Academy Awards for her screenplay writing. The surname reminded me of another acquaintance whom I met in few meetings; Renana Jhabvala, better known for her work with SEWA. Further exploration told me that Renana is one of the three children of Ruth and Cyrus Jhabvala.

Coincidentally, within a few months I had a chance to meet Renana in some meeting or seminar and I told her about the fact which was a new fact to me but obviously, not to her. She smiled at me and said, "Ask Com. Bardhan, why the comrades insisted for such a strange looking cement mesh (jali) in that beautiful building?"

Yes, I recalled. There is a mesh covering entire Ajoy Bhawan; from bottom to top, from rear to front. So one day, I asked Com. Bardhan, why this cement mesh? He responded with laughter and then told us about the attacks Communist Party offices faced at various times including the recent one at the time of Indo-Chinese war in 1962. So when the new Head Quarter of the Party was being planned, the architect Jhabvala was requested to design the building in such a way that the comrades can protect themselves from the outside attacks; and at the same time, they can take some action from inside as well. That is the story of the cement mesh. Why should an architect of that stature agree to do that and also (to the best of my knowledge), not charge any money for the design. The reason was that his father, Shavaksha Hormasji Jhabvala, although not a member of CPI, was one of the founder-veterans of the trade Union movement in Bombay and a friend of Comrade Dange and others. They were all indicted in the Meerut Conspiracy case in 1929.

Ajoy Bhavan from back side

A mesh told me the link connecting Meerut Conspiracy case to 1962 and I was in a state of surprise. Anyway, coming back to the Red Guards, given that a mesh was planned and made, the necessity of Red Guards can be easily understood.

Those who know Ajoy Bhawan, National Head Quarter of CPI, are very familiar with Red Guards. Those who don't know, for them, Red Guards are the Comrades from various places who at one point of time decided to devote their lives to the security of the Head Quarter of the Communist Party of India. There are instances in the past when Party offices were attacked by reactionaries, who have not been in favour of any kind of discussion which involves terms like Socialism, Exploitation, Class struggle, Equality, etc. More recently, fake nationalists tried to first malign and then physically attack the party comrades and offices. In such circumstances, it can be categorically stated that the role and responsibility of Red Guard comrades is of increased importance.

Editor

Com. Jang Bahadur

I came from Bihar to Delhi in the year 1974 in search of a job. I was already married at that time. I was close to the party in Bihar and I became a party member in Delhi in 1984. I was also active in the All India Youth Federation (AIYF) and served as its District Secretary in Delhi. In 1986, I met Com. Bardhan in a meeting. Before that he was a distant personality, a big party leader. I often saw him delivering fiery speeches on many issues even in Bihar, but from a distance.

I was asked by the Delhi Party whether I would like to join the Red Guards as there was a requirement in the Party headquarters. I joined and came here. Com. Bardhan also used to stay in Ajoy Bhawan. I soon realized the softness and kindness of his character, a person who otherwise sent shivers down many a spine with his mere gaze.

I lived in one room of Ajoy Bhawan with my family. My son was born, grew up and got married and became father of two children in his presence. The children enjoyed playing with Com. Bardhan if he was in town, he would certainly come for the birthday celebrations of my grandchildren. He got them admitted in Central School. My granddaughter who was very young, perhaps 4-5 years of age, one day came up to Com. Bardhan and told him, "See, I am going to a meeting". He laughed with amusement.

He was a man of very few needs. His heart was open for comrades and all those who were in need. He used to enjoy good food but never complained if the food was not tasty. Once, we were together in some state where for two days we got cauliflower in our all meals. Local comrades perhaps didn't notice this. Com. Bardhan ate without complaining but I couldn't remain silent. I asked the local comrades tauntingly "Is this the only vegetable grown in your state?" They understood and changed the menu from the next day. But Com. Bardhan didn't complain about anything. He was like a father figure to me. He used to travel a lot on party work. I feel proud of those moments when I accompanied him to various meetings.

These are personal memories and there are many, but above all, he was a towering politician. His humanness, innocent playfulness with kids, were his qualities on one side but his commitment towards the Party was remarkable and inspiring.

Com. Sitaram

Comrade Sitaram has been in Ajoy Bhawan since 1977. We asked him to share reminiscences of Comrade Bardhan with us. He narrated the following:

"Comrade Bardhan used to sit with us and chat everyday near the main gate of Ajoy Bhawan when there was a bigger cabin for Red Guards. He never made us feel that he was a big leader and we had to be careful while talking to him. He had this habit of accepting any suggestion from anybody." Com. Sitaram was referring to small things and not political decisions. We all know how firm and determined Com. Bardhan was when it came to politics. "One day someone mentioned to Com. Bardhan that people come and stay in Ajoy Bhawan free of charge. They should be asked to pay something for their stay. Com. Bardhan discussed it with me. He said we should fix some nominal charges for stay in Ajoy Bhawan. I told him 'what is the use of charging people like this? The party will not get anything from it and it will earn you a bad name. Instead you should give an All-India call for funds and that will raise much more.' Comrade Bardhan accepted the advice and forgot about charges for stay."

The second incident was about watering the plants. Sitaram Ji love plants and is very knowledgeable about them. One day someone said to Com. Bardhan that much water is being wasted on plants. When Com. Bardhan came out of office in the evening Sitaram Ji was watering the plants. Comrade Bardhan told him not to waste water on plants. Sitaram Ji said 'they will die if I don't water them.' Comrade Bardhan replied 'let them die but don't waste water' and went inside again. When he came out again, Sitaram Ji was still watering the plants. Com. Bardhan just smiled and walked away.

Another interesting incident was when Com. Vishambhar Pandey from MP came to Delhi in a rally with 400-450 people. It was cold then and raining. Com. Vishambhar went to Com. Bardhan and asked him for space to stay in Ajoy Bhawan. Com. Bardhan declined saying 'there is not that much space to accommodate so many people in Ajoy Bhawan.' Sitaram Ji told Com. Vishambhar 'you shouldn't have gone to Com. Bardhan for this. I know how to accommodate. Go now to Tilak Bridge and take shelter there for it is raining. Come back to Ajoy Bhawan at night after Com. Bardhan leaves.' At night Com. Vishambhar came back with the 400-450 comrades. Sitaram Ji adjusted them everywhere. 150-200 of them slept in the Meeting Hall upstairs. 50-60 in the library and like this Sitaram Ji accommodated every single one of them. He told them to get up early, bathe and leave before 7:00AM after which Com. Bardhan would come to office. They left before Com. Bardhan came but ofcourse someone complained of all this to him and he came to know that 400-450 people had stayed in the office. But Com. Bardhan never said anything to Sitaram Ji and never mentioned it to him.

That was Comrade Bardhan as Sitaram Ji saw. Ready to listen to everyone and prone to react quickly. But when he knew what was right, he would never hesitate in taking back his words. He led a very simple life and helped many in his personal capacity. He was very caring and concerned about every Comrade. We all loved him.

Com. Amreek Singh

I was working in a Coca-Cola factory in Delhi in the early 1970s when I became a member of AITUC. There was a strike and I was among the victims of the management. I joined the Party in 1974. Delhi Party leaders asked me to take responsibility of the Red Guard and I agreed. That was the time when Com. Rajeswara Rao was the General Secretary. He often used to sit outside Ajoy Bhawan on a stone bench. He was so simple in his looks and behaviour that new comers would never realize that it was Com. Rajeswara Rao who they met outside. I used to accompany him too sometimes during his visits to various places for party work.

Com. Bardhan continued those traditions set by the previous leaders. He never made any comrade feel that he was a big leader. He also used to sit every evening in our cabin reading newspapers or meeting visitors, chatting to us, discussing politics, etc. He was a cheerful person normally. He lived a very simple life. He belonged to a different generation of leaders which included Com. Indrajeet Gupta,

Com. Satpal Dang and Com. Vimla Dang (coincidentally, I belong to the same Amritsar town that was the work field of Com. Satpal and Com. Vimla Dang), who devoted all their lives for the upliftment of the party and the downtrodden. They did nothing for themselves.

Time also gave Com. Bardhan a great name. During his tenure as General Secretary, our Party, CPI, touched new heights of success in parliamentary democracy. Our Party grew in number and strength. He saw the downfall also but never lost hope. He remained politically conscious and tried to do whatever was in his capacity to safeguard the country from communal and corporate forces.

As a person, he was very helpful. He used to avoid attending big political parties which are almost daily affairs in Delhi. But he always tried to attend small functions organised by any party comrade. He used to ask about the problems of fellow comrades and if possible, tried to resolve them. Many people came to him for help and he never disappointed them. All leaders across the party line respected Com. Bardhan. He did not have wishes in life other than the Party. He used to eat in the canteen of Ajoy Bhawan, the same food that other comrades used to eat. He was not fussy at all.

I saw him going to the slums of Delhi where hutment dwellers were devastated because of the demolition drive of the government. He, along with the former Prime Minister VP Singh, went to these poverty ridden localities and fought for them. He also played an important role in the making of pro people laws and acts like MGNREGA, Food Security Act, etc. He was very appreciative of youth, students and women and he always emphasized on study. He used to read a lot.

Com. Lallan Ram

I come from the village Baispura of Rohtas district in Bihar. I got associated with party activities in 1968 when I was perhaps only 12-13 year old. I was not given party membership because of my age. I became a party member in 1976 and in 1977 I joined the Bihar State Party as a Red Guard. The Bihar Party gave me driving lessons and I was given the duty of driving the party car.

I saw Com. Bardhan during his visits in Bihar. He was a powerful speaker. He was a national leader even then. Then I was asked by the Party to drive the car at AITUC central office so I shifted to Delhi in August, 1995. After two years, I went back in Bihar and worked with the Bihar Party again. Later, when Com. Rajappan, who drove the Party Car in Delhi retired and went back to Kerala, I was asked to drive the party vehicle again in 2012. Since then I am working at Ajoy Bhawan.

My tone is considered rough because of the colloquial language I speak. Many party leaders and comrades get angry with me because of the roughness of my language. But it was Com. Bardhan, who understood the emotions and commitment behind this roughness. I even talked in a raised voice with him complaining of work and wages. I said that I wouldn't continue, that I would go back. He didn't get angry with me. Rather he smiled and said "I know that you won't go anywhere. You have remained so long with the Party. I know you won't go." He was correct.

As workers, we find that we don't get sufficient wages and that discontent sometimes comes out. Family pressures are also there. But as a Party comrade, we feel that there is no Party like the Communist Party where a leader of national stature, a General Secretary tries to listen to all kinds of queries of diverse comrades. When I take party leaders to some meetings or gatherings of other political parties, I park my vehicle in the parking lot where other bigger cars of other party leaders are also parked. I wait for my leaders. The other drivers also wait outside along with me. They have bigger cars, better clothes, better salaries but their leaders are not like ours. Our leaders take care of us. The other people can't imagine the respect which we get working with the Communist Party, within and outside.

Once when I was in Delhi, there was some quarrel that took place in my village between two parties. I was also active in Party activities in my village so there were people from other parties who used to feel envious of me. They falsely implicated my name also in the complaint. My family informed me that a case had been registered against me. They were very worried and so was I. I told Com. Bardhan. Generally, he used to stay calm but when I told him about the case, he got very angry. Immediately, he phoned up some comrades. Later, when he visited Bihar for some Party work, he gave a letter to Nitish Kumar for a fair investigation. After that, my name was removed from the charge sheet. He used to take care of every small detail. He never forgot the pain and problems of other comrades and he tried to help everybody in whatever way possible in his capacity. His presence was like a "Badka Baap" (Great Father) in the party and in Ajoy Bhawan. Now, we have his memories with us to keep us going.

Com. Bahadur (Com. Giriraj Kunwar)

I stay in Com. Pallab's room which is adjacent to the room where Com. Bardhan used to stay. He never shut the doors of his room. He always liked fresh air and natural light. He became very weak after he had a stroke in Nagpur. I attended to him almost 24 hours and was conscious for his call. Earlier, he used to go downstairs to the canteen for his lunch, but after the Nagpur incident, he took one chapati and a very small amount of vegetables in his room. I used to give him all his medicines and food. Com. Pallab and all other leaders told me to put aside all other things and pay full attention to whatever Com. Bardhan needed.

My mother-in-law was not well in Nepal and I was getting calls from the family to visit home and so I had to go to Nepal. The very next day after I left, he went into a coma. I came to know of this sad development only after I reached home. And within a day or two my mother-in-law also died. I regret very much that I could not see him when he left us.

He was a very conscious and silent presence around. He used to enjoy watching political debates, news and cricket matches on TV, but his first passion was reading. While reading he was like in a different world.

For some period, I used to run the canteen in Ajoy Bhawan. When he came for lunch, I would serve him one fresh hot chapati and some green vegetables. This I decided for him, he was never particular about food. He never complained or shouted. For us, he was like a father figure. He used to help comrades in need in whatever way possible. Not only financially, but otherwise also. And not only comrades, but whoever came to him. I came to Delhi from Nepal in 2001. At that time I was working with Dey's Medical Company. The Director used to know Com. Pallab very well. That is how I came in touch with AIPSO. I started working with AIPSO since 2003. I came to know Com. Bardhan while working with AIPSO. In April, 2005, I was asked by Com. Pallab to run the canteen in Ajoy Bhawan. That is when I shifted to Ajoy Bhawan.

I experienced his caring nature a number of times. Once when I went home to Nepal in 2015 for holidays, Nepal suffered badly due to earthquake and heavy floods. Thousands of people died. My home was also damaged. When it was over and I came back, comrades at Ajoy Bhawan told me that he used to feel very worried everyday for me and wanted to know the updated situation. He never used to say anything to anybody individually but everybody knew that he was concerned for everyone.

He was a big leader. We have seen many national and international leaders meeting him but this never reflected in his behaviour. I personally requested him once for some financial help when my daughter was getting married, and he didn't disappoint me. Other leaders of the party and organization also helped me.

BRIEF BIO-DATA OF

COMRADE A. B. BARDHAN

Comrade Ardhendu Bhushan Bardhan was born on September 25, 1925 at Sylhet, now in Bangladesh

He joined the Student Movement (All India Students' Federation) in the year 1940, when he entered the University of Nagpur, presently Maharshtra. The same year, in late 1940, he was admitted into the then illegal Communist Party of India.

He became a full-time student organiser, while continuing his studies, and in 1945 he was elected the Secretary of AISF, which he continued to be till early 1948. He was also elected the President of the Nagpur University Students' Union.

He left home and became a Party whole-timer from 1941.

After leaving the student movement, he joined as a Trade Union organiser, and worked amongst power workers, railway workers, textile workers, defence workers, press workers, engineering workers and so on. He was the pioneer in organizing handloom weavers all over the country.

For his activities as a student, trade union and Party organiser, he was arrested several times, and spent a total of about four and half years in jail starting from the 'Quit India' (August 1942) Movement. He was underground for nearly two years, during which he worked as a trade union organiser in Calcutta (West Bengal).

He was elected a member of Madhya Bharat Provincial Committee of the CPI, and then a member of the Maharashtra State Council of the CPI, also a member of its state secretariat, beginning with 1942. He continued his studies which were interrupted several times due to arrests, etc. and obtained degrees in M. A. (Economics) and L. L. B. (Bachelor of Law).

In 1957, he was elected for a five-year term to the Maharashtra State Legislative Assembly.

In 1968, he was elected to the National Council of the Party at its 8th Congress.

Following the Bhatinda Congress in 1978, he was elected to the Party's Central Executive Committee.

In 1982, at the Varanasi Congress of the Party, he was elected to the Party's Central Secretariat. He became the Deputy General Secretary of the CPI in October 1995 (at the 16th Congress), and in August 1996 he was elected the General Secretary. He has been continuously elected as General Secretary till 21st Patna Party Congress held in 2012.

Com. A. B. Bardhan held several leading positions in the Indian Trade Union Movement, as a top official of several unions and National Federations. He became the General Secretary of the All India Trade Union Congress (AITUC) in March 1994, a post which he relinquished on becoming the General Secretary of the Communist Party of India in 1996, which he continued to hold till the CPI Party Congress at Patna in 2012.

He was the brain behind the drafting of the new programme of the CPI which was adopted at Puducherry Party Congress. In this Congress, the Party constitution was amended to create a permanent Programme Commission. Comrade Bardhan was elected first chairman of the Programme Commission. In that capacity he was also a member of the National Executive. Com. Bardhan was a prolific writer. Apart from writing on ideological and political issue, he has written number of books and booklets on problems of Adivasis, minorities, history of working class movement, etc. His last book was on 'Crisis of Corporate Capitalism' that had number of editions during the last one decade.

Joshi-Adhikari Institute of Social Studies

Joshi-Adhikari Institute of Social Studies (JAISS) was established in 1985 in the name of veteran communist leaders and social scientists P. C. Joshi and Dr. Gangadhar Adhikari. It conducts field research, brings out a journal *Social Science Probings,* holds seminars and workshops and publishes books and booklets on various important issues of socio-economic and political importance.

for more details, visit the website - www.jaiss.org.in